Caravans to Tartary

Caravans to Tartary

Roland and Sabrina Michaud

with 81 illustrations, 76 in color, and a map

Thames and Hudson

For our son Romain

Translated from the French
Caravanes de Tartarie
by Jane Brenton

First paperback edition published in the USA in 1985 by
Thames and Hudson Inc., 500 Fifth Avenue, New York, New York 10110
Second paperback edition 1990
English translation © 1978 Thames and Hudson Ltd, London
© 1977 Sté Nlle des Editions du Chêne, Paris

Library of Congress Catalog Card Number 84-51676

Filmset in Great Britain by Keyspools Ltd, Golborne, Lancs.
Printed in Switzerland

'*And coming down from the Pamir where the lost camels call through the clouds.*'

(*A. Malraux*, Les Noyers de l'Altenburg)

Caravaneers.
Seraglio Album, fifteenth century.
Topkapi Museum, Istanbul.

Inset map labels:

Aral Sea

U.S.S.R.

TURKESTAN

Tashkent

TURKMENIA
(KARA KUM)

Amu Darya

Bukhara

Samarkand

Kokand

Tien
Shan

CHINA

Kashgar

TAKLA
MAKAN

Yarkand

SINKIANG

Khotan

CASPIAN
SEA

see large-scale map

Pamir

Hindu
Kush

Kun
Lun

Kara
Koram Mts

Shan

TIBET

IRAN

Herat

Kashmir

Srinagar

Kabul

AFGHANISTAN

Indus

PAKISTAN

Ganges

INDIA

GULF OF OMAN

0   125   250 miles

Main map labels:

U.   S.   S.

Amu   Darya   (Oxus)

Keleft

Qarqin

Shortepe

Dawlatabad

Kaldar

Amu

Andkhoy

Aqcha

Balkh

MAZAR-I-SHARIF

Tashkurgan

Shibarghan

Pul-

Daulatabad

Sar-i-Pul

U. S. S. R.

Maïmana

AFGHANISTAN

Qaïsar

Murghab

Qala-i-Nao

HERAT

——— Roads   = = = Tracks

0   25   50 miles

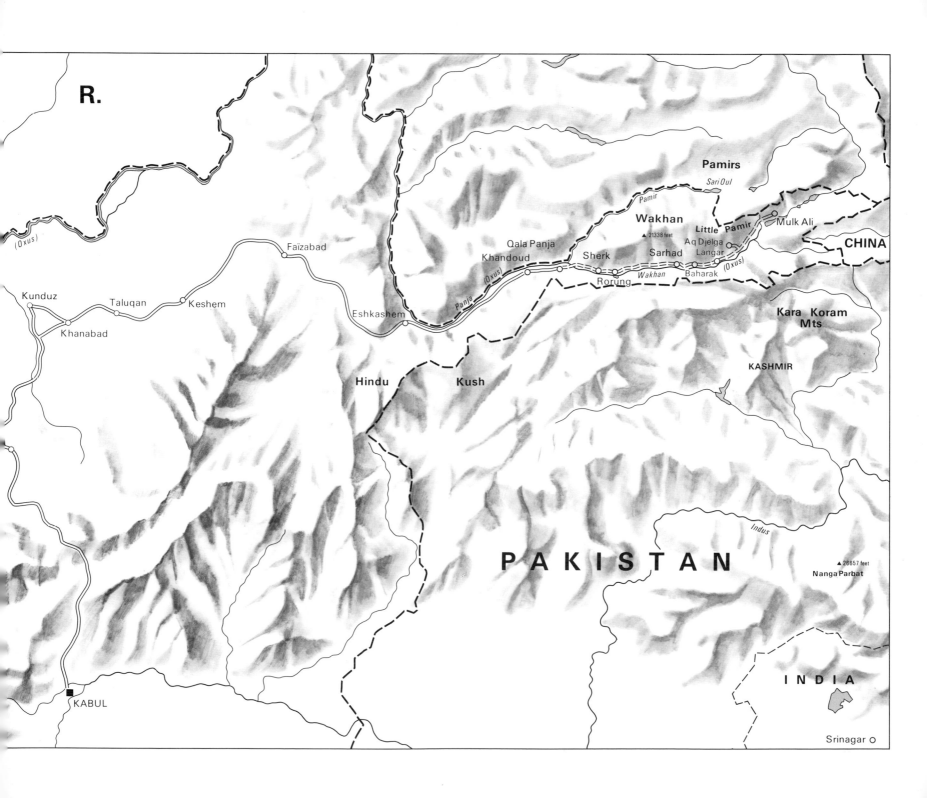

R.

(Oxus)

Pamirs

Sari Oul

Pamir

Wakhan

Little Pamir

Mulk Ali

Faïzabad

CHINA

Qala Panja

Khandoud

▲ 21338 feet

Sherk

Aq Djelga

Langar

Kunduz

Taluqan

Keshem

Sarhad

(Oxus)

Rorung

Wakhan

Baharak

(Oxus)

Khanabad

Eshkashem

Panja

Kara Koram
Mts

Hindu   Kush

KASHMIR

Indus

P A K I S T A N

▲ 26657 feet
Nanga Parbat

I N D I A

KABUL

Srinagar O

Winter caravan on the roof of the world

The still valley lies like a carpet of felt between cold blue mountains. Near a group of dry-stone dwellings seventeen camels are grazing on sweet rush. Five Kirghiz camel-drivers kneel round a wood fire and enjoy bowls of salty tea.

This is the caravan with which we are to travel. Twice each winter it makes the journey from the encampment of Mulk Ali, near the Chinese border, to Khandoud, capital of the Wakhan, taking nine or ten days to cover about 125 miles. Its *raison d'être* is purely economic: dairy products form the basis of the Kirghiz diet and in winter these are in insufficient supply to meet their needs. They are obliged to go to barter their felts and sheep in exchange for grain from the Wakhi peasants living in the lower valleys.

The Kirghiz are of Turko-Mongolian descent and are also indigenous to Soviet and Chinese Asia. At different times in their past they have been herdsmen and warriors, or simply brigands, depending on the fortunes of their rulers and the accidents of history; since the seventeenth century, however, they and their herds have regularly migrated in summer to the Pamirs. Once the route of pilgrims and merchants, the high plateau has become their province.

In the nineteenth century, war between England and Russia led to the partition of the Pamirs between Russia, China and Afghanistan, but the Kirghiz continued to move freely throughout the area, citizens of no particular country. It was after the Bolshevik revolution that the political situation forced several thousands of them to cross from Russia to China, and later from China to the Afghan Pamirs. They became Afghan subjects and settled there more or less permanently, the rich grassland of the high plateaux providing an adequate supply of food for their flocks. The harshness of the terrain ensured that they were left in freedom, without threat of hostile action from the neighbouring peoples, and in addition they were granted exemption from taxes and from military service, on the understanding that they would continue in their role as vigilant watchdogs of the north-east frontier.

It was in the summer of 1967 that Roland and I had made our first expedition to this region. The Kirghiz chief Hadji Rahman Qul Khan had told us then of the existence of these caravans of two-humped camels which travelled in mid-winter, following the route of the frozen river-beds so as to avoid the high snowy passes. Three years of reading and research in Paris failed to confirm their existence, but an exceptional conjunction of circumstances, together with royal permission to travel in the forbidden area, now made it possible for us to embark on our adventure.

Abdul Wakil, the eldest son of Rahman Qul, is waiting for us in Khandoud. He is a squat little man, dressed in black and wearing Russian boots and hat. An important *bey* ('landowner'), he is held in high respect by the peasants, who kiss his hand and address him as *qariadar* ('village chief').

His wealth is indicated by the livestock he owns: 10,000 goats and sheep, 100 yaks, 10 horses and 17 camels. We are to join up with the camels. We ride on horses hired from Wakhi peasants. It is the custom for them to accompany their animals, looking after them and walking alongside, leading them by a rope.

After seven hours in the saddle we reach our first stopping place, Sherk, at an altitude of 9,320 feet, and there we are greeted by a rich landowner. His lively young wife runs up to me, lifts my hand to her lips and kisses it. I kiss hers at the same time and, from her friendly smile, I realize that it is exactly the right thing to do. The next day she presents me with a kind of shortbread for the journey, on a tray covered with a cloth. Knowing that the tray must never be returned empty, I give it back with a packet of tea and a small bottle of perfume.

It is minus 20 degrees Centigrade during the night.

Today we cross the Wakhan River by the Sargaz Bridge, so narrow and lightly built that we have to go over one at a time. Further on, a still riverbed is dotted with giant rushes the colour of rust and honey, reflected in the ice – at times so thin that my horse breaks it with an impatient kick and satisfies his thirst.

Then comes the *jangal* ('jungle'), a word that evokes for us something quite different from these sparse little tufts of yellow grass and occasional thorn bushes. Abdul Wakil goes hunting for hares with his revolver and this evening we will eat *palao* with hare, this being the traditional Afghan dish made with rice and meat or chicken.

The next staging post is Rorung, at an altitude of 10,560 feet; here we stay overnight in a Wakhi house that juts out over the valley where the frozen Wakhan River winds through dark grey sands.

All the following day we spend riding over the peaceful and monotonous plain or splashing through flooded pastures, dotted with iridescent spikes of grass.

Before leaving the Wakhan, the tongue of land that thrusts into Chinese territory, we are able to see in operation the system of barter used between the Wakhi peasants and the Kirghiz caravaneers. First they agree – not without difficulty – a precise rate of exchange: one sheep to 150 pounds of grain (the sheep to be delivered later). Then a large kilim rug is spread on the mud floor so that not a single grain is lost, and a sample of the last harvest is brought. The Kirghiz examine it very carefully, rubbing it between their fingers before accepting it. Abdul Wakil fills a tea bowl, the accepted measure in the Pamirs and the Wakhan, and begins to transfer the grain, bowl by bowl, into the bag held ready by two Kirghiz. Two bowls count as one pound. When the bag is filled it is sewn up with thread plaited by the Kirghiz women and a large needle of the type every caravaneer wears pinned inside his coat. At last the twelve bags are ready. They represent 3,840 tea bowls of grain, and it has taken two hours of reckoning to complete the task.

The caravan is organized on the basis of one camel-driver to three camels, and one horse to each camel-driver. The camels belonging to Rahman Qul are the so-called Bactrian camels, the species also native to the semi-desert regions of China, Sinkiang, Mongolia and Tibet. They are powerful and robust animals, over six feet in height and up to nearly half a ton in weight. They move slowly but surely, often with a characteristic nodding motion of the front hump. The two enormous humps are the camel's reserves and can contain over 200 pounds of fat. Whether they are firm or flabby is the barometer of the animal's state of health. If a camel is tired or ill its humps may diminish and atrophy to the point where they disappear altogether. The camel is the most valuable of all the animals, one camel being worth 8 yaks, 9 horses or 45 sheep – not surprising when one considers that it can carry as much as 600 pounds of merchandise and is also a source of milk, meat and wool.

Well adapted to the severe cold of the high plateaux of Central Asia, the camel has a thick woollen fleece, varying in fineness and softness from one animal to another, a veritable mane running all along the underside of the neck, and thick tufts of hair on the dome of the head and parts of the feet. This wool is both beautiful and valuable, 'so valuable', we learn from one of the camel-drivers, 'that my camels have to be guarded at night to prevent the Wakhis coming and stealing tufts of wool'.

Leaving Sarhad, we enter the valley of the Wakhan River. Initially about 500 yards across, it narrows rapidly until it is little more than a gorge. We ride over the frozen riverbed. The Kirghiz have a very highly developed instinct for choosing the best path, and sprinkle ashes or sand to make the going less slippery. Men, camels and horses follow the path cautiously, in single file. At regular intervals Abdul Wakil bends down to test the river, listening with his head on one side, like a doctor recording a heartbeat. He edges his way past crevasses where the boiling waters are exposed to view. We advance over a crust of ice more than a yard thick. In spite of all the precautions occasional cracks are heard and great fissures split the perfect surface of the ice like streaks of lightning. The walls of the gorge rise up sheer from this icy corridor and are so high that the sun penetrates only when it is directly overhead.

In the early afternoon we are forced to leave the rapidly narrowing riverbed and negotiate a high pass. Aï Bash opens a bag of sand and sprinkles it over a spit of ice so slippery that the camels could not possibly venture on to it. It is a steep climb. The animals hang back and the camel-drivers have to coax them forward. Every fifty yards the caravan halts so that we can get our breath back. Without warning, the last camel collapses right by the edge of the precipice and, driven by blind instinct, crawls, literally crawls, a distance of several yards: risking their own lives the camel-drivers remove its load so that it can get back on its feet.

As dusk falls the mountains loom larger than ever; we wilt at the prospect. 'They are so high', someone says, 'that even the birds cannot cross the summit except on their feet.' Men and beasts set their backs to the side of the mountain.

The summit is reached at last. For an instant these so-called 'sons of the clouds' are silhouetted, black and solid but leaning towards the ground, against the backdrop of the leaden sky.

When I stop for a moment to catch my breath it is the silence, a silence which is total, that makes me giddy. We spend the night in a cave infested with rats. There are many such caves in the valley: firewood or a few branches are stacked against the outer wall for any travellers who may arrive, reassuring evidence of the tacit co-operation that exists among the nomads of the Pamirs. Fire is vital; before matches made their appearance the camel-driver's most precious possession was his *chaqmaq* or flint-lighter, which was worth a horse in exchange.

The route over the next pass, which we cross in the afternoon, is barely wide enough for a horse and skirts the edge of dizzy precipices. I am frightened, but fear is relegated to second place in the struggle to reach the end of the day's journey.

When we arrive, a Kirghiz man emerges from the wealthiest of the yurts (circular felt tents of the Turko-Mongolian peoples), followed by his family. He kisses Abdul Wakil's hand and Roland's.

His wife and daughter run to help me dismount. They lead me inside the yurt, take off my coat, hat, gloves and boots and sit me down by the fire. They smile indulgently when, contrary to the custom, I lie down flat with a sigh of contentment. They busy themselves about the fire, stirring up the embers and putting them to one side, ready to set out the *chogun*, or kettles.

We are in Shakh Dida. It is our first night in a yurt. Our bodies forming a star, feet towards the fire in the centre, we enjoy a good night's sleep in the company of the six members of the Kirghiz family. The thick felt of the yurt is an excellent insulator against cold. The fire is kept going with slow-burning *argol*, or yak dung. Stacked against the willow-wood framework are the possessions of the Kirghiz – materials, bedding and provisions – in bags, cases and trunks. Tea, sugar and salt are the most highly prized of these. Tea is worth so much that each camel-driver carries it about his person in a beautifully embroidered little bag, which is cautiously produced to put tea in the *chogun*. Sugar is so precious that tea is drunk with salt, not sugar, and salt is so scarce that it is used only in tea.

Outside again, the wind bites more cruelly than ever.

We strike north-east, leaving the Wakhan. Only the camels seem unconcerned. They advance silently, scooping up vast mouthfuls of snow with their tongues. The camel-drivers pull their hats down over their ears and foreheads and bury their faces in their fur collars. They do not talk, as though saving all their energy for the battle against the cold.

The altitude is 12,800 feet. It is an extraordinary sensation to feel that we are arriving on the Bam-i-Dunya, the Roof of the World.

By the time we reach the encampment of Aq Djelga I am worn out. The mistress of the house takes off my boots and massages my feet, then takes a wad of wool from a bag and wraps it round each of my toes individually.

In the morning it is snowing. It has snowed all the previous night. Sky is indistinguishable from land and it is hard to be sure if the swaying camels are on the ground or in the clouds. There is nothing to see, no tree, no shelter. Even the faintest sound is muffled. Occasionally we pass an encampment of sleeping yurts guarded by dogs who howl and leap up at our horses. The wind is blowing a tempest, visibility is down to 200 yards, but the Kirghiz move slowly on, knowing instinctively which way to go, while I imagine precipices all around me.

When we reach the end of this leg of the journey we are all exhausted: even Aï Bash, his eyelashes tipped with white frost,

admits he is tired as he ties the camels in pairs, head to tail. Tied up like this they have to bend their forelegs under them in order to lie down, the point of the exercise being to prevent them catching cold from collapsing on the ground as soon as they reach their destination. It is only after two hours in this standing position, called *chapar*, that they are untied and can settle themselves as they wish.

Rather more slowly than usual the caravan moves on towards its final destination. We let the camels and horses crop the grass they instinctively know where to find under the snow. 'One blade of grass from the Pamir is as good as a bale of hay.'

Mulk Ali, the winter camp, looks like a cross between an oasis and a toy building kit. In its three yurts and two mud huts about thirty people live together at close quarters. The nearest neighbour is several hours away on horseback, and the favourite form of entertainment is to exchange visits.

We are to stay in the guesthouse, a huge room, made warm by felt carpets, fur-lined covers and brightly coloured pillows – and most of all by the *bukhari*, the traditional Afghan stove, which has been transported all this way on the back of a camel.

I decide to go and visit the women, starting, as is customary, with Abdul Wakil's first wife, Bibi Orun. My path is blocked by a fierce sheepdog, whose ears have been cut off and who wears a studded collar to defend himself against wolves. Similar dogs belong to each yurt and have to be driven off with stones. Abdul Wakil's yurt houses three women but no children. If in a year's time his third wife, aged only fifteen, also fails to give him a child, then like any averagely wealthy Muslim he will take a fourth wife. I am amazed at the good relations that exist between these women and the way the two younger wifes defer to Bibi Orun, who is forty and treats them like a mother. There is no trace of jealousy between them. I ask Bibi Orun, 'Three women with just one husband, doesn't that cause a lot of arguments?' She laughs and replies that it is no problem at all when the man is just and good, and master of the yurt. 'And of course it means less work for each of us.'

With each day I am increasingly conscious of the monotonous regularity of the various tasks performed by the Kirghiz women. All the morning is spent making bread which, together with the salted milky tea, is the basis of their diet at this season of the year. When the midday meal is over, the afternoon is devoted either to melting ice to provide a supply of water, or to sewing, or very occasionally to their own pursuits. Then once the evening meal has been prepared and eaten they go almost immediately to bed.

We are delighted by the close relationship that develops between us Westerners and these nomads of the steppe. Never for one moment do our hosts fail in their kindness, good spirits and sense of humour. Sometimes Roland goes with them to fetch ice. On the vast frozen expanse of a glittering lake they look like ridiculous dwarfs as they attack the thick ice-pack with repeated blows of an iron bar and fill their bags with the lumps.

The meals offer little variety: mostly meat balls made with minced yak meat, meat soup made from tough leathery mutton, and above all *ash* – freshly made noodles lightly cooked in stock, very difficult to swallow.

The caravaneers have to put up with a very restricted diet while they are travelling, with only two meals a day, morning and evening, so that they do not interrupt the slow progress of the camels. Once back in camp they spend much time simmering their favourite dish, the *qurut*. This is a cheese made of curdled milk, hard as stone, which they slowly stir into water to make a thick paste, adding fat and pieces of bread. At this time of the year it is their only milk-based food, as the yaks do not yield much in winter. We appreciate that the bowl of milk we are offered each day is a generous gesture of hospitality.

One of the women's duties is to milk the yaks, beasts that are a sort of compromise between goat and mammoth, and wear an expression of permanent bad temper. They are however extremely sure-footed animals, not frightened of rivers or fast currents, and capable of great endurance. The acrobats of the mountains, they are less affected than horses by altitude, and are used to crossing high passes of 15,000 feet and over. A yak has only one eighth the value of a camel, and can carry only half as much in weight; but its dung is the best fuel available in the high plateaux of Central Asia, its hair can be used to make stout ropes, its milk is nourishing and its hide tough.

The second and last camel caravan of the year is to leave for Khandoud in two days' time. We shall go back with it.

An air of excitement reigns over the camp: the men shoe the horses, test the strength of the loading ropes, check the felt camel trappings and give the women the provision bags to repair. They are already busy cooking the special bread for the journey.

'It keeps for over a month,' Bibi Orun tells me.

The secret is to work fat into the dough so as to make a kind of shortbread, not unlike ship's biscuit.

Abdul Wakil, an attentive host, notices the deficiencies in our equipment, and supplies us with headgear, felt socks and boots.

The atmosphere is that of an oriental bazaar as the caravan is loaded. We go to say goodbye to the women, whom I kiss affectionately on both cheeks. They return my kisses Kirghiz fashion, on the lips. We end up at Bibi Orun's yurt and are not allowed to leave until we have swallowed every last drop of the bowl of hot sweet milk she has prepared for us. 'It's very good against the cold,' she assures us.

Bibi Orun accompanies me to my horse, helps me mount, and then leads it by the bridle through the camp. As we leave she hands me the reins and says, *Bamone Khoda* ('May God go with you').

We both feel more upset than we would care to admit; but already we are met by the wind's icy blast.

Nomad preparing a meal (detail).
Conqueror Album, Siyah Kalem,
fifteenth century. Topkapi Museum, Istanbul.

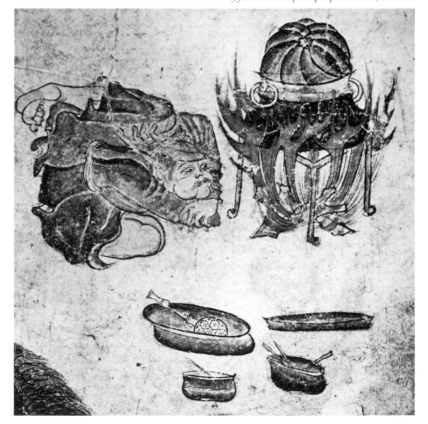

Illustrations

1   Two-humped Bactrian camels. These powerful and robust animals inhabit the semi-desert regions of China, Sinkiang, Mongolia and Tibet.

2   Abdul Wakil leads the caravan along a sandy track in the Wakhan. His horse is protected from the cold by felt trappings.

3   The Kirghiz caravan moves through a valley swept by a sandstorm.

4   Crossing a pass: men and beasts toil up the mountainside.

5   The resourceful Süleyman leads the caravan over a pass.

6   Leaving Sarhad, where the Pamirs begin, the caravan advances into the steep valley of the frozen Wakhan River.

7   The shadows of the caravan of camels are cast on the ice, as sharp in outline as those of shadow-puppets on a screen.

8   A camel has slipped and fallen to its knees, while a camel-driver is straining to help it up.

9   The Kirghiz caravan zig-zags over the frozen river.

10   Sometimes crevasses open up and the boiling waters are exposed to view.

11   The Kirghiz have a very highly developed instinct for choosing the best path for the caravan over the frozen river.

12   The skin round his eyes swollen with cold, Aï Bash arrives exhausted at Shakh Dida.

13   The caravan moves relentlessly on through the white universe of the endless steppe, dotted here and there with spikes of brown grass and black boulders.

14   Evening at the encampment of Aq Djelga. The Kirghiz drive their goats and sheep into a stone enclosure as a protection against cold and wolves.

15   The Bactrian camel can carry as much as 600 pounds of merchandise, and is also a source of meat, wool and milk.

16   The Kirghiz place a particular kind of plant between their lips to prevent chapping.

17   At dusk, the caravan begins the descent of a pass down to the Wakhan River below.

18   In a scene that might be from a Chinese print, the caravan passes across a floodplain where rushes grow in profusion.

19   The cold does not stop Kirghiz children playing out of doors.

20   At the end of one leg of the journey the camels are tied in pairs, head to tail, so that they cannot kneel down; the point of the exercise is to prevent them from collapsing on the frozen ground while still sweating and catching cold.

21   Camels being loaded before the caravan departs.

22   As the last rays of the sun catch the mountain peaks, the camels are untied and settle themselves for the night.

23   The thick felt of the Kirghiz yurt or tent is an excellent insulator against the cold.

24   Over a fire made of yak dung, a caravaneer cooks his favourite meal: a fondue of cooked cheese with pieces of fat and bread.

25   Caravaneers relaxing by the fire in a yurt.

26   The Kirghiz women spend their mornings making bread, the main food in winter.

27   A child born in winter almost never survives; Bibi Jamal lost her child recently.

28   The caravan on the move, at an altitude of 13,100 feet, on the Roof of the World.

29   Shakir's eyes express all the poetry of Tartary.

3

4

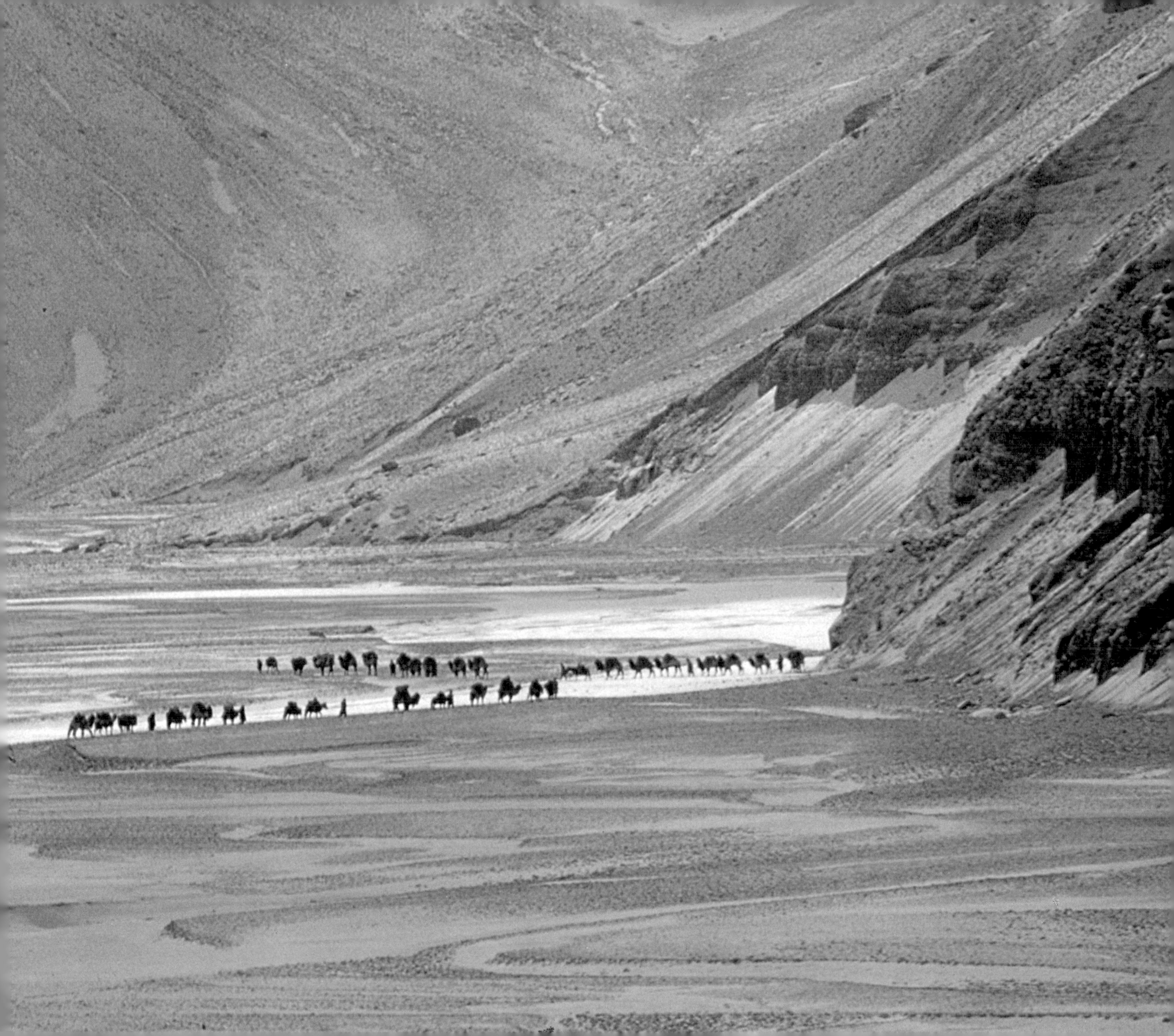

10

13

16

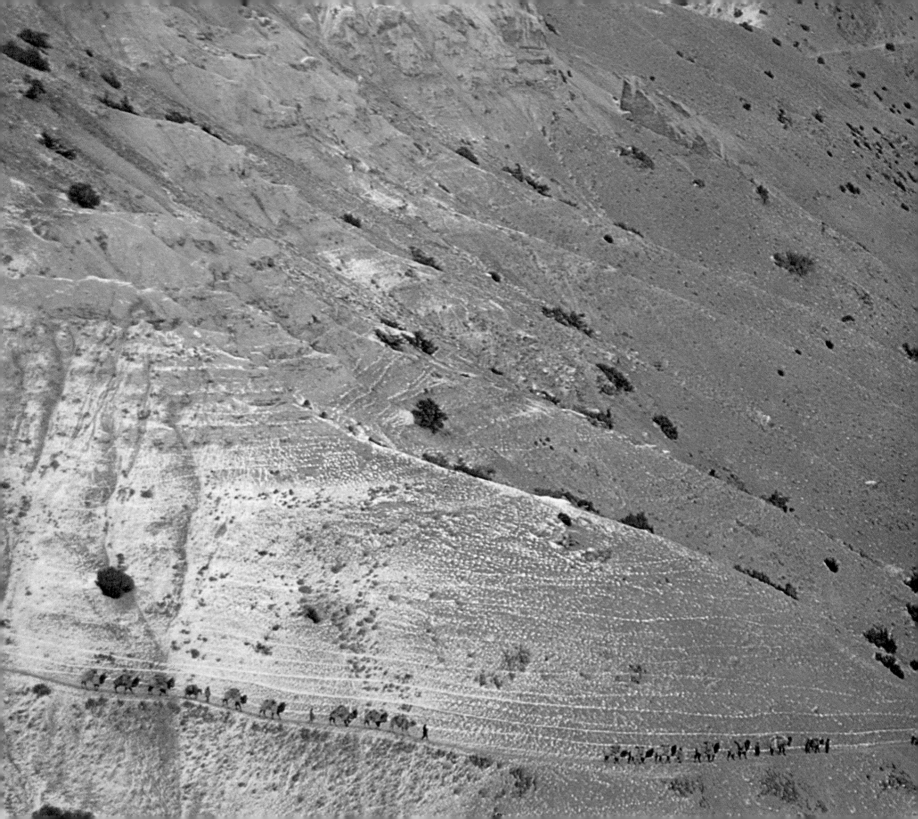

19

27

29

'The earth is hard, the heavens far.'

(Central Asian saying)

Dressage of a horse.
Conqueror Album, Siyah Kalem, fifteenth century.
Topkapi Museum, Istanbul.

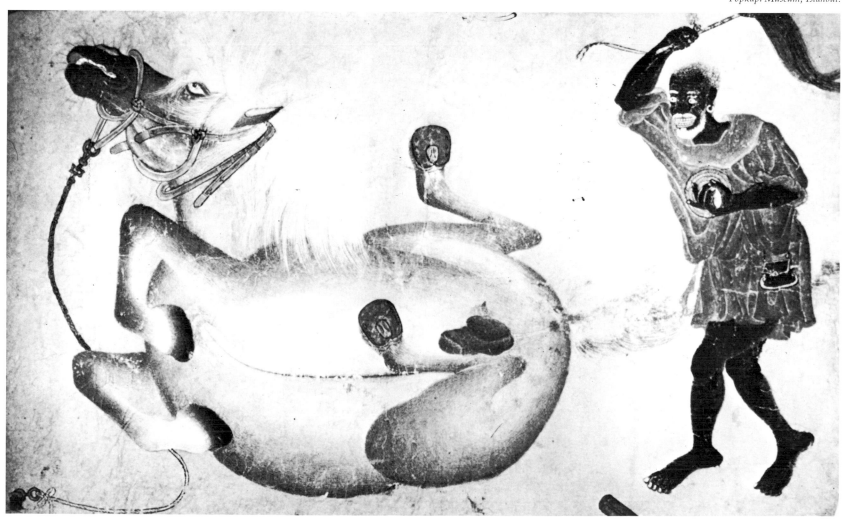

The steppe of the four seasons

The steppe is the Russian name for the vast enclosed area, far from the coast, in the centre of Asia – the Chinese word is *tsao-ti* ('land of grass'). Between deserts of stone and sand its carpet of meagre pastures extends for mile after mile, green in spring, fawn-coloured in summer, sepia in autumn and white in winter, but monotonous and melancholy at every season. It is the steppe that has formed the nomad and given him his taste for freedom and long rides on horseback.

We are exploring the south bank of the Amu Darya River (the Oxus), which for some 800 miles serves as a frontier with the USSR. We are in Afghan Turkestan, the former kingdom of Bactria, researching into the traditions and customs of the Turkmenians, one of the Turkish peoples of Central Asia, in whom we have been interested for the last ten years.

They number about 200,000, and are known as the 'Black People' (*Kara Khalka*), because the colour black (*kara*) is significant in every aspect of their lives. Thus, they inhabit the *Kara Kum* – 'black desert' – together with their flocks of black sheep (*karakol*), live in black yurts (*kara ouille*), and smoke 'Black King' (*kara khan*) or opium.

For centuries the Turkmenians were the dreaded brigands of the steppes. The plague of the caravans, their marauding activities extended even into Persia, from where they brought back not only rich spoils but also prisoners to stock the slave markets of Bukhara and Samarkand. By tradition they were herdsmen and migrated according to the seasons in search of pastureland. Their nomadic life enabled them to escape government control; they paid no taxes in any country and indeed raised their own taxes from the settled population, offering protection in return.

They always resisted Russian domination – the emirate of Bukhara, already a Russian protectorate under the last Tsars, was not abolished until 1920, and in 1930 a rebellion was put down by Stalin. The refugees swelled the numbers of their compatriots in northern Afghanistan. There these brigands of romance, knights whose heroic exploits were celebrated in song by minstrels, turned into peace-loving farmers, reserved, independent and superstitious, maintaining most of their old traditions.

Our route follows a wavering line of telegraph poles, as twisted as climbing vines. Now and then this solitary landmark branches in a dozen directions and winds crazily away into the infinity of the steppe. Whereas in summer we were driving through a rolling terrain where waves of sand made us pitch forward dangerously, getting stuck in ruts a foot deep, now it is winter and we are swimming instead in a sea of mud. A ringing announces the presence of 'ships of the desert'. A bell is always hung from the neck of the rearmost of the five-to-twelve camels that, joined together by a rope, make up a caravan. The bell lets the caravaneer know that all is well with his train of camels. If in his drowsy state he no longer hears the familiar ringing, it means that thieves have cut the rope and are probably at that moment engaged in stealing his animals and their loads. The caravaneer, just like a sailor at sea, is often forced to steer by the stars, for the winds can efface every landmark on his route.

In the past, someone in Zadian told us, fires used to be lit on top of towers, like lighthouses, to guide the caravaneers crossing the Oxus by night.

The camel-driver, like the sailor, is a solitary figure, and his port of refuge is the oasis.

The other voyagers of the steppes are the herds of goats and flocks of sheep. The fleeces of a certain kind of lamb are used for the famous *karakol*, known to us as astrakhan, after Astrakhan, the port on the Volga through which the skins were exported. The fur has enjoyed unfailing popularity over the centuries and was in fashion even at the court of the Hittite kings, as we know from 3,000-year-old bas-reliefs showing warriors with hats and tunic borders in astrakhan. Originally from the region of Bukhara, this breed of sheep is perfectly adapted to the harsh yet dry climate of Turkestan. There is a Persian saying, *Turkestan mulk e paka o pustin*, 'Turkestan, land of fans and furs', which describes rather accurately the extreme variations in temperature, ice-cold in winter, torrid in summer, and ice-cold and torrid within a single day. The sheep possesses great resistance thanks to one unusual anatomical feature, a large store of fat in its tail, which provides nourishment in summer when the ground is scorched, and enables it to maintain its body heat in winter. Some of the lambs are slaughtered either a few days after birth or just before they are born, the latter method producing the silky short-haired *breitschwanz*, the most highly prized quality of fur.

Although our vehicle has four-wheel-drive and we spread branches of tamarisk over the worst sections of the route, we are continually getting stuck, if not in mud then in sand. But with perseverance, and with help from the villagers, we manage to thread our way, following the rhythm of the seasons, through the chain of oases formed by the small towns of Turkestan: Tashkurgan, Mazar, Balkh, Aqcha,

Shibarghan, Andkhoy and Daulatabad; and to visit the string of villages along the bank of the Amu Darya: Kaldar, Djouy, Walkil, Shortepe, Keleft and Qarqin. The Amu Darya varies from 400 to over 1,500 yards across, spreading wide between low crumbling banks, occasionally dividing into a number of channels, then shrinking back between high cliffs. The plain on the southern bank of this great river has for 2,500 years been prized as a highly fertile area, the grain-bowl of all the surrounding deserts and mountains. Long ago it was described by the Greek geographer Strabo as the 'jewel of Afghanistan'. And indeed, when irrigated, the land is extremely fertile and yields cotton, cereals, vegetables and fruit in abundance.

Set in a landscape of sand or steppe with stunted vegetation are the villages, within which each dwelling has a number of subsidiary buildings grouped around the central house: stables, grain and cotton storehouses, guesthouse, and of course the traditional yurt.

Irrigation canals make it possible to cultivate the parched loess soil (wind-blown sand): we pass through fields of corn, sesame, barley and lucerne, and orchards whose delectable fruits were already being praised by poets 2,000 years ago – there are mulberries, almonds, apricots and pomegranates, and above all grapes and melons, the latter being regarded as the 'sultan of fruits'. It is said that there are melons in Turkestan which, when fully ripe, burst at the sound of horses' hooves.

Elsewhere there are fields of cotton with snowy white flowers – precious because the cotton seeds provide an edible oil, the stalks can be used as fuel, and the oil-cake is fodder for the flocks.

We reach the village of Daulatabad, a place of infinite sadness. Clouds of crows black out the sky. We pass through muddy streets, full of closed shops, with a few stocky figures hurrying home. The hungry wolves feel very close.

The bazaars of Central Asia

At the crossroads of the ancient routes from India to Bukhara and from Persia to Chinese Turkestan, the small town of Tashkurgan exemplifies the typical bazaar of Central Asia, all that remains of the great caravan trade of past centuries.

Not long ago, skins and furs were being bartered for tea from Yarkand. Today one can still walk about in the muffled quiet of the *Tim* – an octagonal brick building, its cupola decorated on the inside with stucco and pendentives set with porcelain saucers and bowls.

This is the centre, the point towards which all the many covered passages of the bazaar converge; it is occupied now by merchants selling embroidered caps – the sort of caps which the men wind their turbans around, the complicated patterns and brilliant colours varying according to their village of origin.

Throughout northern Afghanistan bazaars are held twice each week, on Monday and Thursday. On those days, from all four corners of the steppe, there is an influx of donkey-drivers, caravaneers and camel-drivers, come to sell their products and buy whatever they need.

An animated crowd floods through the narrow streets, the shops, caravanserai (or resthouse), baths and teahouses. The different crafts are formed into guilds, their role fixed within a static universe that has not changed for centuries, in which every part is perfectly organized and articulated within the whole: everything in its place, every being in harmony with his surroundings and the sky above.

Weavers, carders, smiths ... all have achieved a perfect beauty and precision of gesture.

Jewellers are helped by their young apprentices to melt down silver coins or set cornelians – the stone said to protect sight – in the amazing Turkmenian pendants, bracelets and collars.

A *patragar*, or 'mender of crockery', sits tailor-fashion, holding between his two feet the pieces of a broken teapot, tied round with thread. With a drill pointed with an ordinary gramophone needle, he bows away like a violinist, piercing holes in the porcelain. He then makes clips from little pieces of wire and fits them to the broken pieces, fastening them with a local cement of lime and egg.

In the street where the cobblers work we are astonished at the variety of leathers used in the shoes (no distinction is made between the right and the left foot). There are low-heeled shoes with turned-up toes and soles of camel leather; black indoor boots in supple goat leather, without heels; children's boots of tan cow leather; green grained-leather shoes for women, of horse's or donkey's hide; high-heeled *boz-kashi* boots.

The bazaar assails our senses: smells of dung, bread and wax, of kebabs, salt and leather, cummin, almonds and myrrh; colours – calico of orange-red nacarat, muslins of purple amarant, soft saffron-coloured silks; sounds – the braying of donkeys, cries of caged rock-partridges, the hubbub of the crowd.

In the tiny shops all the wares of Central Asia are spread out on display: water-skins, which can be inflated and secured under rafts used for crossing rivers; wooden chests decorated with brightly coloured motifs cut out of waxed cloth, and ornamented with large-headed nails; wicker cages; musical instruments; rare herbs and condiments; enormous blocks of rock-salt brought by caravan from Andkhoy; pyramids of sweet and bitter oranges from Djelalabad.

Sitting behind their scales, abacus and accounts book, which is bound like a copy of the Koran, the enigmatic merchants with their narrowed eyes, patient and wise, seem ready to wait an eternity. Yet who can say what will be left in twenty years time of these Turkmenian markets, with their astrakhan, their grain and their carpets?

A hairy dervish chants and twirls an incense-burner which emits clouds of sweet-smelling smoke, designed to rid our minds of Evil. We offer thanks in the form of the two oranges we have just bought.

This picturesque character is the *isfandi*, a dervish of the order of Naqshband, which was founded in the fourteenth century. Using hot charcoal he burns grains of *isfand*, or wild rue, whose smoke is said to ward off evil influences. In this fashion he proceeds from shop to shop, and everyone thanks him with a coin or some gift in kind.

The midday call to prayer of the *muezzin* on the top of a minaret – here records have not yet replaced the human voice – reminds us that it is lunchtime. We feast ourselves on kebabs of liver with onions and a round of hot bread. We also order the traditional rice dish with meat or chicken. Then we relax in one of the numerous teahouses. There we realize to the full what the oasis must mean to someone who has come from the barren desert of the steppes.

Following the Muslim custom, we remove our shoes before sitting down on the carpets that cover the mud floor. Not a single local woman is to be seen of course. We are immediately shown to the best place, right next to the stove. There we can see the whole room. The walls are covered with paintings in a primitive style, of pomegranate flowers, melons and birds, and are decorated with framed pictures of the King and Queen of Afghanistan, the Kaaba at Mecca, the sanctuary of Mazar-i-Sharif, and quotations from the Koran done in beautiful calligraphy, such as the *basmala*: 'In the Name of God the Clement, the Merciful'.

Written up in big letters is the Persian saying: *Khush Amaden* ('May you be welcome').

Hanging from the ceiling rafters are wicker cages, one containing a songbird, a yellow-beaked blackbird, and the other a partridge of the type used as a fighting bird, with money wagered on its chances. There are also mirrors, a *dambura* (a two-stringed musical instrument) and a gramophone playing Indian and Pakistani music.

An atmosphere of extraordinary charm and grace fills the room.

With a subtle play of light and shade the sun's rays filter through the screens of branches and rush matting, to fall in blue stripes on the gold and silver of the ewers and samovars. A murky light bathes the faces of the customers, wrapped in their *chapans*, coats fit for kings, and wearing turbans as majestic as crowns. They look as though they have stepped out of a Persian miniature.

As soon as we are settled, the *bacha* comes to take our order; the only drinks available are refreshing green China tea or warming black Indian tea.

Sitting before his two gleaming samovars – one in use, the other still heating – the owner prepares the drinks. He puts a pinch of tea into the little Japanese teapots before filling them up with boiling water. These he then hands to the *bacha*, together with bowls and a saucer of powdered sugar or *noquls*, a sort of mulberry-shaped sugared almond.

As we sip our scalding tea, we observe and we listen. The customers hand round the hookah as they exchange greetings and news. One question keeps coming up, *Bazar et garm ast?* (literally: 'Is your bazaar hot?') – an enquiry as to the state of business, which leads on to a conversation about the price of grain, on which everything else depends, even the price of carpets. There is talk of the next *boz-kashi* (game played with a goat- or calfskin filled with sand) or the next marriage: 'Shah Mohammed has to pay out another seven thousand afghanis to his future father-in-law if the wedding is to take place, never mind the eighty-seven thousand he has already given him.'

It is in the teahouses that the interested traveller can pick up a lot of information about the life of the country.

This particular teahouse looks out over a caravanserai with a large courtyard crowded with animals. Surrounded partly by walls and partly by buildings, some with an additional storey, this mud construction is typical of the market towns of Turkestan. Its function is to accommodate travellers, animals and merchandise. To penetrate inside is to share the private life of the caravaneer, for, after a long journey through the desert, this is the refuge where he finds rest and food for himself and his animals.

A donkey-driver comes to leave his mount, on his way paying the *seraiwan*, or resthouse attendant, for the donkey, which he himself ties up to a wooden stake planted in the ground. He then draws a bucket of water from the well and slowly quenches his thirst. Fodder is provided by the *seraiwan*; that is the source of his income, together with what he can earn from selling the droppings of the animals left in his care. Sheep dung, for example, is used for cooking food, while cow and donkey dung is formed into flat cakes and dried, and is much appreciated as a fuel because its smoke drives away the mosquitoes. At about four o'clock the peasants and merchants begin to leave the bazaar, in order to be back in their villages by nightfall. The caravanserai empties, but new customers arrive in the form of caravans loaded with flour, fodder, cotton, blocks of salt or charcoal; in winter these caravans travel over the steppe by day but stop for the night at a resthouse. At night the bazaar is closed and is guarded by the *chaokidar*, or 'watchmen'. They are armed with sticks and call out to each other with long modulated cries to make sure that they are all alert.

At the hour when, according to the saying, 'you can no longer tell a black thread from a white one', the watchmen hang paraffin lamps on the shutters of every third or fourth shop. When I am woken in the night by a howling dog, I am reassured to see these guttering little flames shining in the night.

A Turkmenian wedding

Big flakes of snow are falling; the tiniest blades of grass are metamorphosed. In this unreal atmosphere a number of chilly figures are busy with the camels, loading each one with a *kajawar*, the sort of panniers that are hung from the animal's pack-saddle. One of the camels is decked out in an elaborate harness with beaded pom-poms and little silver bells; the *kajawar* has a lightweight dome placed over it, and this is covered with a cloth, a number of rugs, pieces of silk and talismans. Some of the men drag a carpet to the door of one of the yurts. There is a symbolic struggle with the occupants. The bride is being seized from her father's house.

For weeks now I have been trying to get to know some of the women, and for weeks provincial governors or their deputies have attempted to please me by introducing me to Turkmenian village leaders, usually the *rish safid* (or 'whitebeards'), who can guarantee both my respectability and that of the women I visit. But the meeting is always disappointing. I feel I am in a sense being imposed on them and the relationship is false from the outset. Then, out of the blue, in the most unexpected of places – a *hammam* or 'public baths' – I am pitched straight into the private life of a young Turkmenian girl, and what is more, I am invited to a wedding.

My new friend Zulfiya lives in the *chol* ('desert'). In spite of the very precise directions given us by her father, we can see no sign of a village in this desert of grey sand dunes. Not a trace of a path. At frequent intervals we stop and climb the dunes to scan the horizon. Smoke in the distance puts us on the right track. As if by magic we come on an encampment of yurts.

We have arrived just in time to see the bride being carried on a carpet to the most elaborately decorated *kajawar*.

With a slow measured gesture the women in their long robes wish her prosperity and happiness as she passes by. Spreading their hands to the sky, the men say a prayer. The camel slowly leaves the camp, followed in caravan by the other camels, which by now are carrying the rest of the women and girls. In this manner the Turkmenian bride leaves her family: seated on a carpet which she has woven with her own hands, she is led to her husband in her future home. Like frosty haloes, the silver jewellery of the bride's companions tinkles joyfully, mingling with the sound of the tambourines which they beat with gusto, while singing: *Kilin aljak, kilin aljak* ('We are bringing the bride, we are bringing the bride').

Young woman with a musical instrument. Seraglio Album, fifteenth century. Topkapi Museum, Istanbul.

Impossible to know what the bride herself can be thinking about a husband who is still a virtual stranger. As soon as she arrives she will be carried, still on her carpet, inside a white felt yurt – the smoke gradually blackens the felt, hence the word *kara ouille* ('black room') which the Turkmenians use for their tents. Surrounded by her friends, she will remain there until the evening. Not until after the evening meal will the husband enter the by-then deserted tent, preceded by the *mullah* (the interpreter of Muslim law) and his two witnesses.

'Have you chosen this girl to be your wife?'

'Yes.'

'Did you hear?' he will ask the two witnesses.

'Yes.'

Then the *mullah* will ask the girl the same question, but the custom is for the witnesses to fail to hear her reply the first time. She must repeat 'yes' more loudly in response to the priest's question. He will then bless the newly wedded pair and congratulate them, and then husband and wife will find themselves alone together for the first time.

The next morning, the two old women responsible for establishing the girl's virginity must be asked, 'Has the boy become king?' Offered 'as a slave' on the day when the marriage is proposed, the suitor becomes king once it is consummated. The truth is that he becomes not so much king as absolute monarch, and the revenue from the carpets the girl produces becomes his rather than her father's. The man's wife may be as richly decked with precious stones as his horses are with silver-plated bridles; but the horse at least enjoys freedom and respect, while she is a prisoner and suffers from neglect. Her domain is the house, where she works without pause, weaving and bearing children. Sometimes her husband takes a second wife, then a third – but whether there are one or four the same fate awaits them. If they are to live harmoniously together they have no choice but to get on well, never saying a word out of turn. Their smiles are reserved, their laughter rarely heard; they behave like queens, and their gestures are those of fairies. And the carpets they weave so untiringly do indeed seem to have magic in them: those scenes of gardens, in deep muted reds, through which flow streams bathed in light and shade, the representation of the paradise on earth described in the Koran. Their inner strengths, their joys and their sorrows, are all incorporated into what they weave.

More literally, it is the central Islamic tradition of the nomads that is expressed and handed down in these carpets. They are the furnishings of Turkmenian life, and the harmony and intensity of their colours, and the rhythm and balance of their geometric designs, symbolize a profound sense of unity.

I like the peacefulness and serenity of these women. And if the carpets reflect their inner life, then I can even like their submission. Could the carpets themselves be so beautiful if they did not reveal a beauty of soul?

The riders of the steppes

Furiously galloping horses emerge from whirlwinds of dust, sparkling in the sunlight. The arid fawn-coloured plain vibrates under their fiery hooves. Whip in hand or between their teeth, the riders surge over the burnt plain like a horde avid for conquests. Suddenly the limitless expanse of the steppe seems to shrink. The horses gallop towards us, nostrils dilated, wild-eyed, whinnying. They are growing so big! I shut my eyes so that I do not have to see them sweep me away and crush me in their headlong dash – and forget entirely that I am ensconced on the roof-rack of our car. The fantastic game that is being enacted in front of us is the famous *boz-kashi* (in Persian: 'catch-goat'), which is still played by the Turkish peoples of Central Asia on Fridays and feast days in winter.

The day before a game a goat, or these days more frequently a calf, is ritually slaughtered; its entrails are removed and it is then filled with sand, sewn up and soaked all night in cold water, to give it body and weight. The feet are cut off to make it harder to get a firm grip on an object which may weigh between sixty and eighty pounds.

The following day, the skin is taken to the chosen playing area and put in the centre of a circle marked out with quicklime and called *hallal* ('circle of justice'). The players, who vary from six riders to an unlimited number, gather round the circle, then at a signal from the 'leader of the *boz-kashi*' they launch themselves at the headless calf. A goal is scored by grabbing hold of this 'ball' and galloping away with it, right round a pole that has been erected far away on the steppe, then carrying it all the way back again and throwing it into the circle of justice. Simple enough in theory, but what scrums and turns of speed, duels and duets, are needed to achieve it in practice! The more familiar we become with this virile and tough sport, the more finesse and subtlety we discover in it.

A true enthusiast, I do not merely watch the game, I live it. The scrum jostles against our vehicle and the rear lights shatter. The riders tussle furiously over the calf. Flank to flank, the horses rear at every lash of the whip on their rump, stand vertical on their hindlegs in their efforts to reach the skin, plant their hooves on the calf so that their own rider can grab hold of it, and even bend their forelegs to help him do so. These are the best horses in the world, both powerful and robust, fast and supple, beautiful and intelligent. Over the centuries their fame spread from China to Italy – the Chinese used to call them 'celestial'. Since the eighth century the celebrated thoroughbred Arab horses have all come from this region, though there is nothing arab about them except their name. They are worth a fortune, and it is only the great *beys* who can afford them and can maintain stables on the necessary scale.

For this purpose they employ specialists whose knowledge has been handed down orally from generation to generation. These people train the animals, breed them, and follow their progress from one *boz-kashi* to the next, in order to see how they perform and find the most effective combination of horse and rider.

It is for glory, not for gain, that the *beys* spend a fortune on their horses, and when one of them emerges the victor from a tournament, he is so delighted that he promptly spends yet more money on feasts in honour of the winning rider and his mount.

Suddenly a rider falls and rolls like a cat in the dust to prevent himself being trampled underfoot. He quickly remounts and, face streaked with blood and dust, plunges again into the hellish circle.

Impassive, proud and haughty, he lashes out indiscriminately at man and beast to clear his path.

'Who is that?' I ask our Uzbek friend Mardan Qul.

'It's Hakim d'Aqcha, one of our best *chopendoz* ['crack rider'].'

His name means wise, so he is the one who should win. I will him to win.

All at once the circle yields. A rider breaks away, clutching the calf with one hand, and to get a better grip lodges it between his thigh and his saddle. Hakim is on to him at once. One moment he is galloping level with his rival, the next he launches his body forward and dives. He is holding onto his horse only by the heel of his boot. Flying through the air, his two hands outstretched, he tears the calf from his startled opponent, then straightens his arched body and throws the skin on his horse's neck. The rest of the pack follow at his heels.

For a moment I am transfixed by the sight of the flowing mane of his horse, and fall into some kind of trance. It is as though it is no longer a calf he is holding but a distraught girl, her face hidden in her veil. It is not the *chopendoz* who are in pursuit but the girl's parents, trying to get back what belongs to them. Could that be the origin of the *boz-kashi*? A form of training for abducting a shepherd-girl on horseback and outdistancing pursuit? As one daring exploit followed another, it would mean that only the bravest and indeed the most astute of the men would marry, for of course the girl's parents would in the end give him legally what he had taken for himself, rather than be dishonoured.

Scrums form and disperse like clouds of birds swooping down on their prey. As the riders move into the distance, the steppe returns to its real size.

The *chopendoz* perpetuate the heroic equestrian traditions of the Turkmenians, a reminder of the centuries of marauding that took them as far as Persia.

These are the élite of the riders, who have taken part in hundreds and hundreds of *boz-kashi* and whose names are known to the most obscure village or herdsman, because their fame extends to every corner of the land.

They are heroes who possess mental as well as physical courage, wisdom as well as strength, cunning as well as skill. They can gallop for a whole day on their horses. They are the descendants of the Huns of Attila, of whom the chronicles say 'that they dared not dismount from their horses even to sleep', who founded the empires of the steppes under war-leaders such as Genghis Khan or Tamburlaine. It was men such as these whom Alexander's soldiers christened 'Centaurs'. There is a saying: 'When the Tartar is separated from his horse, what can he do but die?'

Hoofbeats that make the earth tremble, muffled whinnyings and wild cries announce the approach of these men.

Pedlars, fools and children hastily dash away from the playing area. The tumult and excitement intensify. Here they are – Hakim moves out of the pack. A man offers him a drink from a spouted flask. As the water flows down his throat, the prominent veins betray his state of tension. Beads of sweat collect under his *talpak* – the small round cap with a crown of astrakhan and brim of fox-fur or wolfskin.

A rider with a fiery looking mount approaches, dismounts, and holds the horse for Hakim while he slides nimbly from his own tired beast and straddles the new one.

In the course of a tournament a *chopendoz* may change horses as many as four or five times.

Hakim at once rejoins the packed ranks of the players. They are battling for possession of the calf with Murad, a demonic figure with a broken nose who clings energetically to the *boz*. Like lightning the lash of a whip splits his cheek, and pain makes him loosen his grip. With an iron fist, Hakim grabs the skin. If he is to keep it he has no choice but to launch himself at the watching crowd and force his way through. He does not hesitate and darts forward, followed by the raging horde.

The crowd scatters in confusion with cries of terror. The charge passes like a whirlwind behind the stand. No one is hurt.

The harsh notes of a stringed instrument help to calm feelings down, and the group disrupted by the intrepid riders close ranks once more. To one side, one of the *chopendoz* winds felt strips round his calves – a protection against cold as well as blows – then adjusts his silk sash and tucks his whip inside.

Elsewhere horses are resting, stripped of saddle and harness, circling slowly under the watchful eye of a groom before rolling in the dust, all four hooves in the air.

The care that is lavished on a *boz-kashi* horse is almost unbelievable. Even at the moment it is born it is not allowed to 'fall' to the

Mongol horseman.
Seraglio Album, fifteenth century.
Topkapi Museum, Istanbul.

ground, for, they say, 'that would break its wings'. Then, so that it will grow a soft, shiny coat, its mother is given ten eggs a day. And, the ultimate privilege, until the age of three the horse is allowed total freedom, for his sole destiny in life is the *boz-kashi*. Only then is he saddled and trained to accept a rider. His mane and tail are never cut and are washed every day. His hooves are never shod. The real training does not begin until two years later.

Today's *boz-kashi* is the last of a three-day tournament. It is being held in honour of the circumcision of the two sons of a rich landowner from the village of Qaou Tchin in the province of Shibarghan, and he has invited the best *chopendoz* in the area.

Over these three days there have been dashes and collisions, falls and quarrels, scrums and breakaways, attacks and feints; amid the drama of the galloping horses, the feats of equestrian skill have defied belief. Suddenly, above the hubbub of the mêlée of horses, rings out the harsh, strong voice of the leader of the *boz-kashi*: *Akher urlaq* ('End of *boz-kashi*'); then, in the same guttural tones, comes the announcement of the reward for the last goal to be scored – a gold *tila*, a Bukhara sequin worth one thousand afghanis (about eleven pounds sterling). Redoubling their energy and courage the riders swoop on the calfskin, and the most vicious scrum yet develops, each player trying to find a way out. Whips crack, horses paw the ground, men yell. A bitter smell of sweat and the lingering taste of dust prick our throats. The nervous stamping of the horses raises clouds of dust. Strangely, Hakim is keeping out of the scrum. But I can see his hawk profile, his narrowed eyes, his body with its muscles tensed as though it possesses all the energy in the world, his horse relaxed and confident.

Suddenly he stands on his stirrups, arches his torso, and with a predatory cry throws himself into the scrum. He emerges at once in a prodigious bound. The rest are at his heels but the chestnut in its streaming coat seems to fly. Just a few seconds' lead on the pack enables him to be first round the post and then to charge full tilt at the goal.

Hallal! Hallal! he cries, raising his arm in a gesture of triumph.

In a few minutes the vast steppe becomes grey, immobile and voiceless. In the austere silence there is no hint of the spectacle that for four whole hours has filled it with the smell of sweat and blood.

Illustrations

45 Hanks of wool that have just been dyed a deep blue are hung out to dry on a tree by a dyer.

46 Portrait of a man; the Uzbeks, another of the Turkish peoples of Central Asia, live side by side with the Turkmenians.

47 Portrait of a woman from Sar-i-Pul.

48 Water-skin merchant in Andkhoy. Some of these skins are used to provide buoyancy for rafts crossing rivers.

49 The last big covered bazaar in Turkestan is in Tashkurgan; to this day it is run on a system of craft-guilds.

50 This butcher in Mazar-i-Sharif also runs a restaurant. Turkmenian kebabs, which consist of cubes of mutton roasted in the animal's own fat, are appreciated as far away as the capital, Kabul.

51 Uzbek barber in Andkhoy; he is shaving his customer's head, as demanded by Muslim tradition.

52 Knife-grinder in Tashkurgan.

53 Repairer of crockery. He is highly skilled at mending bowls and teapots.

54 In the teahouses, which are furnished with carpets, a supply of water is permanently on the boil in copper samovars. Pots of warming black tea or refreshing green tea await the traveller.

55 It is in the teahouses that news is exchanged and that one can hear the storytellers and singers.

56 Jura Eshan, the falconer, shares his bowl of tea with his falcon. The village huntsman, he trades his kill for food and clothing.

57 In the caravanserai a Turkmenian relaxes and smokes a hookah.

58 An encampment of yurts in the steppe south of the Amu Darya.

59 Turkmenian woman with her distaff. The little triangle of cloth fixed on her headdress is to ward off the evil eye.

60 Turkmenian women gathered in a yurt, making tea.

61 Bibi Aqnika is a married woman. Her high headdress indicates her married state.

62 A wedding caravan in the steppe. 'We are bringing the bride!' sing her friends as she is carried, hidden beneath a canopy to meet her future husband.

63 In the husband's village, the women await the arrival of the bride.

64 The men have just helped the bride onto her camel and hidden her beneath the canopy.

65 The bride quickly joins in the day-to-day activities of her new family. Here Turkmenian women are relaxing with bowls of tea before returning to their weaving.

66 The pattern of jewels and the colour of the headdress worn by a Turkmenian woman indicates the tribe to which she belongs. Here, the headdress of a woman from Bukhara.

67 The boz-kashi, the spectacular game played by the riders of the steppes, recalls the equestrian feats of a former age.

68 A chopendoz ('crack rider'), lead-weighted whip in hand, prepares to launch himself into the fray.

69 On occasions, the riders have no choice but to force a path through the crowd – who panic and flee in all directions.

70 The spectators follow the game, either on horseback, or from a makeshift grandstand.

71 His expression tense, a chopendoz quenches his thirst.

72 The game is a ferocious struggle to gain possession of the stuffed skin of a headless calf. The winner is the rider who manages to get hold of it and carry it to the far end of the playing area and back, before throwing it into a circle marked out with quicklime on the ground.

73 Still played every Friday in winter in the steppes of northern Afghanistan, the game recalls the invasions of the galloping Mongol hordes of Genghis Khan and Tamburlaine.

74 In the scrum of men and horses, the chopendoz grasp their whips between their teeth in order to leave their hands free to grab the calfskin.

75 It is a common occurrence for a chopendoz to have his cheek split by the lash of a whip.

76 The game over, the steppe is quiet again as the riders return to their villages.

33

43

44

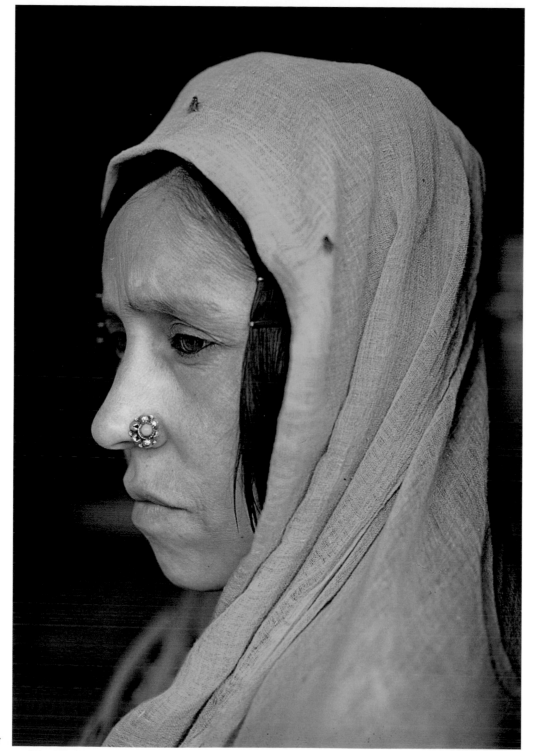

47

54

59

68